The War
in the Pacific
From Pearl Harbor to
Okinawa, 1941–1945

There is an old saying that you can always spot
a real soldier, he will try to catch up on sleep at
every opportunity. This G.I. is using his pack
for a pillow and is wrapped in the standard
raincoat. His helmet has been camouflaged with
paint and his canvas leggings have been cut
down for comfort. On his ammo belt hangs a
canteen and a three-pocket grenade carrier.
(27th Div. Okinawa). (NA-SC)

On the right, a rifle grenadier with 1903 Springfield rifle (note the rubber boot on the rifle stock) helps a casualty in the one-piece 'frog-skin' camouflage jungle suit. The casualty carries the M1928 Thompson submachine-gun with 50 round drum magazine. The grenadier wears the standard green HBT fatigues with the early gas mask bag slung in front of him. It was very unusual to see this bag actually used to carry a gas mask. (27th Div.7/43, New Georgia) (NA-SC)

THE G.I. SERIES

THE ILLUSTRATED HISTORY OF THE AMERICAN SOLDIER, HIS UNIFORM AND HIS EQUIPMENT

The War in the Pacific

From Pearl Harbor to Okinawa, 1941–1945

Jonathan Gawne

Greenhill Books
LONDON

Stackpole Books
PENNSYLVANIA

Greenhill Books

The War in the Pacific: From Pearl Harbor to Okinawa, 1941–1945 first published 1996 by Greenhill Books, Lionel Leventhal Limited, Park House, 1 Russell Gardens, London NW11 9NN
and
Stackpole Books, 5067 Ritter Road, Mechanicsburg, PA 17055, USA.

British Library Cataloguing in Publication Data
Gawne, Jonathan
The War in the Pacific: From Pearl Harbor to Okinawa, 1941–1945. – (G.I.: The Illustrated History of the American Soldier, His Uniform & His Equipment; Vol. 6)
1. World War, 1939–1945 – Campaigns – Pacific Area
I. Title
940.5'426
ISBN 1-85367-253-X

Library of Congress Cataloging-in-Publication Data available.

Designed and edited by DAG Publications Ltd
Designed by David Gibbons.
Layout by Anthony A. Evans.
Printed in Hong Kong.

DEDICATION
This book is dedicated to the original men of Company 'F', 102nd Infantry Regiment. This unit defended Christmas Island against a Japanese invasion that never came, while fighting a brave war against monotony and boredom.

ACKNOWLEDGEMENTS
The majority of images used in this volume are from the National Archives in College Park, Maryland. The author wishes to extend his thanks to the entire staff of the Still Photo Branch for their assistance in this project. Thanks are also extended to the countless veterans who put up with questions about the minutiae of their life during World War II.

ABBREVIATIONS
NA-SC	U.S. Army Signal Corps Collection, National Archives
NA-NY	U.S. Navy Photo Collection, National Archives
NA-MC	U.S. Marine Corps Photo Collection, National Archives
TH	Tom Heinonen
GG	George Ghastly
JG	Jonathan Gawne

In order to assist the reader in tracking the differences in uniforms and equipment throughout the Pacific war, information on the unit, date, and location has been added to as many captions as possible. Unfortunately, this information was not always recorded by the Signal Corps.

THE WAR IN THE PACIFIC FROM PEARL HARBOR TO OKINAWA 1941–1945

The stereotypical view of the war in the Pacific is that of U.S. Marines storming the beaches of small tropical islands. There is an element of truth in this, but the war in the Pacific was much more far-reaching. Almost every possible type of terrain was fought over in the Pacific Theater, ranging from the cold Aleutian Islands off the coast of Alaska, down the California coast and across the empty South Pacific Ocean to Australia. In the South-West Pacific fighting took place in thick, steamy jungles and on mountain slopes. Farther west men fought in China and Burma – where the mountains were the outposts of the Himalayas.

Twenty-two U.S. Army divisions (including one cavalry and one airborne) saw combat in the Pacific, as opposed to only six Marine divisions. The Army supplied countless other support troops to run a logistical system that stretched halfway around the world. Unlike Europe, the Pacific Theater, for the most part, lacked even a basic infrastructure. These soldiers had to build everything, roads and shelter included, from scratch. The U.S. Marines played an important role in the Pacific, but the average G.I. – the foot soldier of the U.S. Army – has been overlooked too often. Volumes have been written on the Marines and airmen in the Pacific, but very little on the U.S. Army.

When the Japanese attacked Pearl Harbor, Wake Island and the Philippines in late 1941, the Allies already had decided that when war came the main thrust would be against the Germans in Europe. This decision meant that the Philippines did not receive vitally needed supplies that might have prevented its capture by the Japanese. The principal effort in the Pacific would be to defend the bases at Hawaii and in Australia until enough men and material could be provided to go on the offensive.

Australia was vital to the war because it was the most developed base of operations west of Hawaii. The defense of this continent involved the Allies in a long and bitter campaign on New Guinea, just north of Australia. It was in New Guinea that the Army realized it was totally unprepared for war in the jungle. The khaki cotton shirt and trousers were not suited to combat, and the green fatigue uniforms made from herringbone twill cloth (HBT) quickly became the standard combat uniform. In 1938 the Army had begun to replace the blue denim uniform that constituted fatigue (work) clothing. Yet many of the obsolete blue denim uniforms were still in use up to 1942.

The main changes in Army equipment during the first few months of the war were the replacement of the bolt action M1903 Springfield rifle with the semi-automatic Garand Rifle, and the replacement of the flat M1917A1 helmet with the now-famous M1 steel pot. The main infantry pack, the M1928 haversack, was a peacetime design that forced the soldier to roll his belongings up in a blanket, then fold the haversack flaps around this roll like an envelope. The M1928 haversack was replaced very late in the war by the M1944 pack – a design based on a Marine Corps issue item. Officers and mechanized troops were issued the M1936 suspenders, to which the M1936 musette bag could be attached as a small pack.

Before the war many items such as towels, handkerchiefs and underwear were white. As soon as fighting broke out in the Philippines, the men realized that white attracted attention in the jungle and began to dye their white articles with local berries. Later on, soldiers in Australia would use coffee to darken white fabrics. Eventually the Army began to make everything olive drab, but it took a while before white items worked their way out of the supply system.

An attempt was made to develop a jungle uniform and specialized equipment. Most of this new material made its appearance in mid-1943. A one-piece jungle suit was produced in a camouflage pattern with the official nickname of 'frogskin'. This blotchy pattern was reversible from a green side (for jungles) to a brownish side (for use on sun-baked beaches). The jungle suit was designed to protect the wearer from insects, while keeping the suit from fitting too tightly against the skin, which would cause chafing. An internal set of suspenders supported the weight of the suit. The main problem with the one-piece design was that a soldier had to disrobe to perform bodily functions. After a year the jungle suit became obsolete and was replaced by a two-piece suit cut on similar lines to the regular green HBTs, but in the 'frog-skin' camouflage pattern.

The camouflage uniforms were a problem because they worked well when the troops remained immobile, but once they started to move it made them stand out. Because the Americans were normally on the offensive and had to keep moving, the majority preferred to wear the regular green HBTs. The official color of the HBTs was changed from a light green to a darker color (olive drab #7) in 1943. The HBT uniform was changed a few times throughout the war. The HBT jacket had four patterns – the first had a band at the bottom with two buttons in front and small breast pockets; the second did away with the band, and used large unpleated pockets; the third put pleats in the large pockets; and the fourth shrunk the pockets to a standard shirt size. The trousers were originally cut normally, but later were given large pockets on the thighs.

Shoes were a major problem in the tropics. The standard service shoe was designed to be worn with a canvas legging. In some areas these leather shoes lasted only ten days before they rotted away. Men unloading supplies on coral beaches only got four days' wear out of their shoes before they wore out. A canvas and rubber 'tropical boot' was developed, and was well liked by soldiers, but it provided poor support for long-distance marching. After the war it would be issued as a substitute tennis shoe. In 1944 an improved combat boot, with buckled leather cuff, began to be issued to the troops. A similar design was developed just for distribution in the tropics, but was never produced.

The basic organization of the U.S. Army stayed the same throughout the war. The basic combat unit was the rifle squad of twelve men. The squad was commanded by a sergeant, and was armed with eleven rifles and one Browning Automatic Rifle (BAR). A rifle platoon was commanded by a lieutenant and was composed of three squads. A rifle company was made up of three rifle platoons and a weapons platoon of two light machine guns and three 60mm mortars.

Three rifle companies and a heavy weapons company, with eight heavy machine guns and six 81mm mortars, made up a rifle battalion (which included a headquarters group containing three 57mm anti-tank guns). A regiment was made up of three rifle battalions, an anti-tank company of nine 57mm guns, a cannon company of six heavier artillery pieces, and a headquarters and service company.

An infantry division was composed of three infantry regiments, three 105mm artillery battalions, one 155mm artillery battalion, a reconnaissance troop, one engineer battalion and one medical battalion. Support services were provided by a signal company, a quartermaster company, an ordnance-maintenance company, an MP platoon and a headquarters unit provided support services. A corps was composed of a variable number of divisions, and an army was made up of a variable number of corps.

Each corps and army headquarters had independent units which they could attach to a division to add to its strength. A corps could decide to attach extra engineer, artillery or armor units to a division to provide more of a punch for a specific attack. There were no armored divisions in the Pacific, but independent tank companies and battalions were attached to units that needed help breaking through Japanese defenses. For most of the war the light M3 Stuart was the most commonly used tank. It was not until late 1943 that the heavier M4 Sherman was sent to the Pacific.

In late 1942 the army started to make a few offensive moves in select areas. At Guadalcanal the Marines had landed first, and a few U.S. Army divisions came in after them to help push the Japanese off the island. What had become apparent was that air power would be the controlling factor in the war, and most of the battles would be fought over control of locations suitable for the support of an air base. When they learned that most Japanese soldiers would not surrender, the Allies decided that unless a Japanese-held island was needed for the advance on Japan, it would be by-passed and the Japanese garrison starved out.

The climate of the South-West Pacific caused a number of medical problems for the troops. Any cut would immediately become infected. Skin left wet from swamps and rain would grow various funguses. Illnesses such as dengue fever, scrub typhus and malaria sapped the strength of both armies. Atabrine pills, a synthetic form of quinine, prevented the worst attacks of malaria but tinted the skin a yellow color. Atabrine, possibly more than any other factor, allowed more men to remain in the front lines rather than be evacuated as casualties.

The Pacific soldiers had to fight not only against the Japanese and the environment, but also against the decision to defeat Germany first. Because of this policy, there were no bakery, bath, salvage or graves registration companies in the Pacific for the first two years of the war. These functions were essential, so men had to be taken off the front line to perform such duties, which drained the combat units of strength. There was a severe shortage of all kinds of equipment in the Pacific, from bread ovens to landing craft, that was not dealt with until mid-1943.

Food always posed a problem in the Pacific because of the harsh demands on storage. Most food containers disintegrated quickly in the tropics. The C-ration, sealed in tin cans, stood up to the climate much better than the cardboard-boxed K-ration. The monotony of the same three C-ration meals (meat and beans, meat and vegetable hash, meat and vegetable stew, along with biscuits that had been enriched with vitamins at the expense of taste) finally was reduced by the addition of more C-ration menus. A special jungle ration was developed and manufactured on Hawaii that included chocolate, cigarettes and hard candy. This special ration was issued for the first couple of days of an amphibious landing and proved quite popular.

The turning point came in 1943 when the specialized jungle equipment began to be issued to the troops. A jungle hammock, surrounded by mosquito netting and under a waterproof cover, allowed the men to sleep in comfort above the ground. This hammock could not be used in combat areas where men had to sleep in their foxholes, but it was popular in the rear areas. Unfortunately, these hammocks wore out very quickly and had a useful life of only 45 days.

Other special equipment included inflatable rubber bladders that could either be used to store water, or to provide extra buoyancy when crossing streams. A larger and more useful pack was made in both olive drab and frog-skin camouflage. This jungle pack was a rectangular bag that could hold a great deal more than the obsolete M1928 haversack. Another essential item was the machete, supplied with a sharpening stone, for cutting through the tangled growth of the jungles.

A special tropical uniform was developed out of a thin olive drab-colored poplin. This lightweight two-piece suit was tested in limited numbers in late 1944. It was accepted for issue in mid-1945, but a lack of production facilities delayed manufacture until the end of the war rendered the garment unnecessary. Sadly, photographic evidence of this limited uniform is almost non-existent.

Landing craft were unable to cross the coral reefs that ringed many of the islands, so the amphibious tracked vehicle known as the alligator was developed to bring troops right up to the beach before they were exposed to fire. The Japanese altered their tactics and set up elaborate defenses inland, rather than try to stop the Americans on the beaches. The war became a deadly job of digging the Japanese out of their bunkers and foxholes.

It was not until 1944 that the Army started to use a chemical treatment to rot-proof all canvas items. This extended the life of everything from tents to radio covers. The old-style raincoat was finally replaced with a poncho. The Army had started to issue the Marine Corps camouflage ponchos in 1942 on a limited basis. It was not until much later that the olive drab army-style poncho was developed and issued to the men in the field.

By the end of 1943 the Allies had essentially destroyed the Japanese threat to Australia and New Guinea. The Americans had also made progress farther to the north in the Gilbert Islands where Marines had captured Tarawa after a bloody fight, and the 27th Division had taken Makin. The Japanese toehold in Alaska had been broken when the Army had retaken the island of Attu. The withdrawal of the Japanese garrison on Kiska went unnoticed by Allied Intelligence, and the invasion proceeded as planned, although without any defenders.

In 1944 the Allies went over to the offensive in the Pacific theater. Enough supplies had already been stockpiled in Europe, so the Pacific began to receive a greater amount of material. After the landings in Normandy and southern France, most of the landing craft in Europe were transferred to help out in the Pacific. With a great deal of tropical fighting experience, the Army realized that not all of their special jungle equipment was useful. The one-piece camouflage suit was altered to a two-piece jacket and trousers set. Many troops simply cut down their one-piece jungle suit into a camouflage jacket to wear with standard HBT trousers.

There was a characteristic pattern to most of the fighting in the Pacific. During the day the Americans would attack, but at night they would dig foxholes and stay in them. The unwritten rule was that anything that moved at night was the enemy. If an American thought there was a Japanese soldier near by he would not use his rifle but toss a grenade. This kept the Japanese from locating his position by the muzzle blast.

Slowly the two main Allied thrusts made headway. In the South-West Pacific, General Douglas MacArthur was moving toward the Philippines, while Admiral Chester Nimitz in the Central Pacific was advancing on the Japanese homeland. In July 1944 the Japanese were finally eliminated from New Guinea, and in October the invasion to liberate the Philippines began. At the end of the year the Pacific Theater, instead of Europe, received the bulk of reinforcements and supplies from the States.

Once the Philippines were captured, the Army moved to the invasion of Okinawa. This was seen as the final stage before the invasion of the Japanese home islands. Once airfields were constructed on Okinawa, the American Air Force would be able to exercise total control of Japanese air space and bomb the country at will. The Japanese recognized the threat, and attempted to drive off the Americans with kamikaze attacks. Okinawa was finally declared secure by the Allies in June.

Before plans for the final invasion of Japan could be carried out, the two atomic bombs were dropped. Japan officially surrendered on 2 September 1945. For many years after, Japanese soldiers came out of hiding throughout the Pacific. Some peacefully surrendered on hearing the war was over, some died in a final suicide attack, and a few remained deep in the jungle, unable to accept defeat.

FOR FURTHER READING

Bergerud, Eric. *Touched by Fire*, New York: Viking Press, 1996.

Cowdrey, Albert. *Fighting for Life*, Free Press, 1994.

George, John, *Shots Fired in Anger*, NRA Press, 1987.

Hammel, Eric. *Guadalcanal: Starvation Island*, Pacifica Press, 1987.

Windrow and Hawkins. *The WW2 G.I.: U.S. Army Uniforms 1941–45 in Colour Photographs*, London: Windrow and Greene, 1993.

Zedric, Lance. *Silent Warriors of WW2*, Pathfinder Publishing, 1995.

Above: Bayonet fighting is being practiced by men wearing different versions of the fatigue uniform. One man wears the pre-war blue denim fatigues, while the others wear the green herringbone twill uniform. Blue denim was phased out between 1938 and 1942. In 1943 the color of the HBT uniform was changed to a dark green. The fatigue uniform was originally designed for work details, but became the standard hot-weather combat uniform. (NA-SC)

Right: These soldiers in Alaska are guarding an outpost in the Aleutian Islands. They have the M1917A1 flat helmet, which was replaced by the famous M1 helmet in 1942. Two soldiers wear a tan to white reversible parka and heavily greased 'blutcher' boots designed for use in the Arctic. The Aleutians, in contrast to other Pacific islands, have a very cold and windy climate. (NA-SC)

Above: Men of the 32nd Division practice amphibious operations somewhere in Australia in July 1943. They are wearing the HBT fatigue uniform and the inflatable lifebelt. They are boarding an LCR (Landing Craft, Rubber). Of special interest is the camouflage pattern painted on their helmets. This was very rare in Europe, but appears to have been fairly common in the Pacific. (NA-SC)

Opposite page, top: The 4.2 inch chemical mortar was designed for gas and smoke shells, but could also fire high explosive and white phosphorus rounds. With a range of over 4,000 yards, it filled the gap between the lighter 81mm mortar and heavier artillery. It was not normally found in an infantry division, but could be attached to one if the commander needed some extra power. (NA-SC)

Opposite page, bottom: This 75mm pack howitzer is manned by a Marine crew on Bougainville in 1943. The gun had a range of almost 10,000 yards. The Marines wear camouflaged fabric helmet covers and trousers. Neither item was issued in any quantity to Army units during the war. Note the captured Japanese flag in the center. (NA-NY)

Above: Members of the 'Scouts and Raiders' unit are shown training for beach landings at Fort Pierce, Florida. The Scouts and Raiders were an élite unit of men whose job was to provide detailed reconnaissance of invasion beaches. They landed weeks before an invasion to map out the landing area. They are wearing the 'frog-skin' pattern jungle suit, knit wool caps and inflatable lifebelts. (NA-SC)

Left: This man displays some of the special equipment designed to protect soldiers against mosquitoes. He wears an insect headnet, special anti-mosquito gloves, and holds a bottle of insect repellant. His HBT uniform was produced late in the war, as it uses plastic buttons rather than the traditional blackened metal ones. None of these items were widely used in combat. (NA-SC)

Above: A Pacific island has been reproduced on this Hollywood set for a training film on fighting in the jungle. World War II was the first conflict in which training films were used extensively. The U.S. Army drafted a number of Hollywood technicians and put their talents to good use making films on every imaginable subject. They enabled men from New York City, the Arizona desert and the mountains of Vermont at least to see what a jungle looked like before being shipped to New Guinea. (NA-SC)

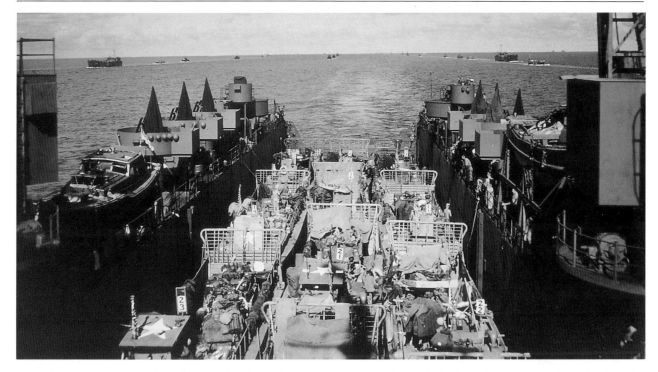

Opposite page, top: A member of the Marine Corps (in the camouflage helmet cover) helps an Army aidman administer blood plasma to a wounded soldier. The use of blood plasma, as well as complete blood transfusions, did more to save casualties than any other medical advance. This fluid kept up the wounded man's blood volume – which prevented him from going into shock. (NA-MC)

Opposite page, bottom: General Douglas MacArthur was in command of the South-West Pacific Area, which included Australia, New Guinea and the Solomons. He is shown here, in his bullion-embroidered cap, on his triumphant return to the Philippines Islands. Although hailed as a hero by American civilians, he was not as well liked by the men he commanded. It is very clear from this photo that the combat troops wore the darker HBT fatigues, while the rear echelon officers wore the khaki cotton uniforms. (NA-SC)

Above: This specialized ship is an LSD (Landing Ship Dock) – a floating dry dock. The main deck is filled with pre-loaded LCVPs (Landing Craft, Vehicle, Personnel) ready for the invasion of Morotai. When the time comes, the LSD will fill its bilge tanks with sea water and sink lower into the ocean, thus flooding the main deck, allowing the LCVPs to sail off and proceed to the beach. After the invasion the LSD will be used to repair smaller vessels. (NA-SC)

Below: The LVT-4 (Landing, Vehicle, Tracked) was an improvement over the original 'alligator', as this version has a door in the rear. Previous models forced the men to disembark by climbing over the top. This could be hazardous if a Japanese machine-gun was shooting at the vehicle. On land it could travel at 20 miles per hour, but less than half that in the water. (NA-NY)

A training center in the U.S.A. made this large map to keep men up to date on the progress of the war. The trainees wear the later dark green HBT fatigues, while the instructor (possibly a returned combat veteran) wears the khaki cotton shirt and trousers. For most of the war the majority of replacements were sent to Europe. By the winter of 1944 the emphasis had switched to the Pacific. Meanwhile, the armies of the European theater were expected to keep up to strength with casualties returning to duty. (NA-SC)

Wearing the pre-war blue denim fatigues and the M41 field jacket, this infantryman examines a C-ration can. At his feet are both meat and bread C-ration cans, and the chocolate D-ration in its waxed cardboard box. The garrison cap with regimental distinctive unit insignia would have a light blue piping to indicate that his branch of service was the infantry. (29th Infantry Regiment, 2/42, Fort Benning) (NA-SC)

Right: Captain Art Wormuth, one of the defenders of Bataan, is shown here with his Filipino aide. He carries an M1928 Thompson submachine-gun and a pistol. The khaki cotton shirt and trousers were the hot-weather combat uniform until it was replaced by the green HBT fatigue uniform. Many of the Filipino troops were fiercely loyal to the Americans, and continued to fight as guerrillas until the liberation of the Philippines in 1945. (4/42, Bataan, PI) (NA-SC)

Above: Soldiers wearing the khaki cotton uniform and overseas hat display typical equipment of the 1941 period. The flat helmets and bolt action rifles would soon be replaced by more modern equipment, but the rest would stay the same for most of the war. These are mechanized troops, as they carry the M36 musette bag instead of the M28 haversack. (808th TD Bn, 6/42, Camp Robinson) (NA-SC)

Right: Cavalrymen wearing the flat M1917A1 helmet practice deploying the 37mm anti-tank gun. This gun was not powerful enough for use against most German tanks, but did perform well against the lighter Japanese armor. Each battalion had three 37mm guns in the anti-tank platoon until they were replaced in 1943 by the heavier 57mm gun. (107th Cavalry Regiment, 5/42, Ft. Ord) (NA-SC)

Above: In a simulated beach assault a squad paddles an assault boat across a river. The men wear the khaki cotton uniform, along with standard M1938 canvas leggings, and the early fiber helmet liner as headgear. This fabric-covered liner (identified by the thick edge) deteriorated quickly and was replaced by a sturdier plastic one. (41st Div. 11/42, Australia) (NA-SC)

Below: Artillerymen attempt to maneuver a 105mm howitzer through thick Australian jungle. The lack of decent roads in the Pacific limited the use of standard artillery pieces. Each division had three artillery battalions, each with twelve of these guns, and a fourth battalion of twelve 155mm howitzers. (41st Div. 12/42, Australia) (NA-SC)

Right: Men of the 32nd Division prepare to board a ship in Australia on their way to New Guinea. The central figure carries his two barracks bags, that were replaced later in the war with a single duffel bag. Although the other men carry the M1 Garand, his weapon is the 1903 Springfield bolt-action rifle. One man in each squad was still issued this rifle because no grenade launcher had yet been developed for the M1 Garand. (32nd Div. 11/42, Australia) (NA-SC)

Right: The crew of a 75mm 'pack' howitzer on maneuvers in Australia. This gun was called a 'pack' howitzer as it could be broken down into six mule loads for transport over rough terrain; this made it extremely useful in areas where there were no roads. The gun saw action in the Pacific in the regimental cannon companies organized in late 1942, as well as many Marine Corps artillery units. (32nd Div 3/43, Australia) (NA-SC)

Opposite page, top: Given only a few trails in the jungle, these men move supplies at Guadalcanal by hauling a boat up a river. By this time the green HBT fatigues were considered the standard hot-weather combat uniform. One man has cut his trousers down to make unofficial shorts. The extra canteen hung from the cap chain was a common field expedient. (1/43, Guadalcanal) (NA-SC)

Opposite page, bottom: An Americal Division soldier examines a .25 caliber Japanese rifle. He is wearing the first-pattern one-piece HBT suit, which was disliked by combat troops as they had to disrobe to take care of bodily functions. He also wears the early-pattern cotton khaki fatigue hat. Note that he has taped his dog tags together to prevent them from making noise. (Americal Div., 12/42, Guadalcanal) (NA-SC)

Below: With no port facilities on Guadalcanal, soldiers were obliged to hand-carry all supplies off landing craft such as this LCVP (Landing Craft, Vehicle, Personnel) and stack them on the beach. A large number of men were needed to unload the boats, thereby gravely weakening many combat units. Even while performing this kind of heavy labor, most men are wearing their canvas leggings. Until 1943 there was a serious shortage of such landing craft in the Pacific. (12/42, Guadalcanal) (NA-SC)

Bottom: Emplaced in a secondary defensive line on Guadalcanal, this 37mm anti-tank gun is well protected in a sandbagged bunker covered with palm logs. A special 'canister' round converted this cannon into a very large shotgun which was highly effective against Japanese charges. There was a tendency for men to strip down in the middle of the day, but the ever-present malaria-carrying mosquitoes made long sleeves necessary at night. (12/42, Guadalcanal) (NA-SC)

Above: This photograph of a brother and sister meeting in Australia illustrates the Australian-made wool battledress jacket issued to some American personnel. It was produced temporarily at the start of the war when American uniforms were in very short supply. The WACs carry the three-snap lightweight gas mask bag, and wear the M36 musette bag as a backpack. (7/44, Australia) (NA-SC)

Below: Most of the WACs sent to the Pacific worked in offices far from combat. Their typical uniform was this khaki cotton blouse and skirt. Ties were mandatory in all but the hottest areas. In the U.S. Army, ties were always tucked into the shirt between the second and third buttons, unlike the Marines who always wore their ties outside the shirt. (1/45, Australia) (NA-SC)

Above: In the field most WACs wore either the one-piece female HBT suit (left) or the two-piece female HBT suit (right). The WAC on the right holds her HBT jacket and wears the woman's cotton shirt; the other wears the round cotton summer WAC hat. Supplies of female uniforms were frequently difficult to obtain, so it was common for women to wear small-sized male uniforms. (6/43, USA) (JG)

Left: This 32nd Division infantryman has just been sent by air from Australia to New Guinea. He carries 80 rounds of ammo in his belt and an additional 48 rounds in each of the two fabric bandoleers. The burlap helmet cover is very unusual and seems to have been made for this division just prior to being shipped out to New Guinea. It does not appear in photographs long after the division has been in combat. The dark color of the HBT uniform appears to indicate that it has been over-dyed a darker shade. (32nd Div, 12/42, New Guinea) (NA-SC)

Right: These medics from the 32nd Division prepare to haul supplies into the New Guinea jungle in late 1942. The medical supplies are strapped to the first model 'Yukon' packboard. The headband is to help stabilize the load. The men wear the first model one-piece HBT suit with the HBT hat. (14th Portable Hospital, 12/42, New Guinea) (NA-SC)

Right: These infantrymen eat a last meal of C-rations before heading out to combat on New Guinea. Of special interest is the full M1928 haversack seen at left. This was a cumbersome pack which was originally designed in 1910 for peacetime use. It was one of the most hated and ineffective items of equipment in World War II. The twin-snap first-aid pouch just in front of it is surplus from World War I. (32nd Div, 12/42, New Guinea) (NA-SC)

Above: As units moved into combat, extra gear was discarded and the soldiers took on a less uniform appearance. This squad shows a mixture of helmets and HBT hats. A few men have already discarded their leggings. Canvas leggings, though awkward, did serve to protect the lower leg from insects and thorns. In jungle areas any cut would rapidly become infected, so it was important to protect as much of the skin as possible. (32nd Div. 11/42, New Guinea) (NA-SC)

Below: A medical unit in Port Moresby ready to enter the jungle. Some of the fabric helmet covers have been camouflaged with hand-painted patterns. The only marking to identify them as medics is a small section of the Red Cross armband pinned to their sleeves. In the Pacific, the bright red crosses of medical personnel offered an easy target for Japanese snipers. (32nd Div. 11/42, New Guinea) (NA-SC)

Above: The six 81mm mortars in the heavy weapons company were the largest support weapons that could be easily hand-carried by the crew. This mortar crew in New Guinea is firing the standard high explosive round – still painted in the bright yellow peacetime coloring even though it is April 1943. The loader provides an excellent view of the pockets on the first-pattern HBT trousers. (41st Div. 4/43 New Guinea) (NA-SC)

Right: Now in the front lines, these men have stripped down to the bare essentials. Their belts carry only ammunition, water and first-aid equipment. The 1928 Thompson sub-machine-gun was considered an ideal weapon for the jungle. The high rate of fire allowed men to spray the thick vegetation without having a specific target. The New Guinea jungle was perhaps the worst environment in the world to fight in because of its density, heat and humidity. (32nd Div, 12/42, New Guinea) (NA-SC)

Right: Testing of different camouflage uniforms started in 1942. These men wear four different versions of camouflage that were tested in the U.S.A. At left is a traditional hunter's 'ghillie suit' made from strips of burlap. Next is the 'frog-skin' jungle suit that eventually became the standard American camouflage uniform. Note the cammo helmet cover for the flat 1917A1 helmet. On the right is a suit of burlap bags developed out of sniper experience on the Western Front in World War I, and a standard HBT suit that has been hand-painted. (1942, U.S.A) (JG)

Left: Major General Horace Fuller, commander of the 41st Division, models his unit's solution to jungle fighting. The 41st took their HBT uniforms and dyed them in the vats of an Australian brewery. The result was this rather effective field expedient camouflage. The general wears no insignia on his uniform or helmet. By regulation no insignia was to be worn on the fatigue uniform. (41st Div. 2/43, New Guinea) (NA-SC)

Right: Two officers of the 41st Division relax en route to combat. They wear the dyed camouflage HBT uniform with undyed HBT hats. Although the ammo belt appears to have been dyed as well, there is no evidence that this unit attempted to camouflage their web gear. The officer at left wears a lieutenant's bar on both hat and jacket collar. These emblems would be shifted to below the collar as soon as warning was received of Japanese snipers. (41st Div.1943, New Guinea) (NA-SC)

Below: The 105mm howitzer was the primary artillery piece used in the Pacific, with a range of 12,000 yards. There was no need for longer range on most of the small islands. The crewmen are wearing the first-pattern HBT jacket and trousers with the khaki cotton fatigue hat. This lighter-colored hat was the forerunner of the similarly designed HBT hat. (1942, Australia) (NA-SC)

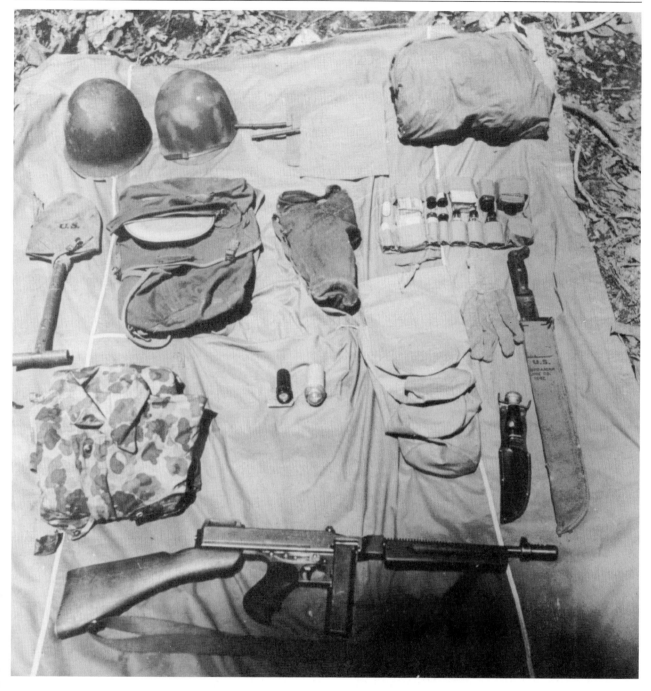

Opposite page, top: The 'frog-skin' pattern jungle suit was designed to be worn without any underwear or other clothing. An internal set of suspenders carried the weight of the suit and kept it from chafing the wearer. It was reversible with one side bearing a greenish pattern for jungles, the other a brown pattern for sun-baked areas. The major problem was that soldiers virtually had to remove the uniform to perform bodily functions. (1944, New Guinea) (NA-SC)

Opposite page, bottom: Although the jungle was always damp, drinkable water was a rare item. Local sources of water could carry any number of tropical diseases. Until the issue of water purification tablets later in the war, most squads carried an extra canteen full of chlorine. A capful of this chemical would make one canteen of water safe to drink, but leave it with a foul taste. (41st Div. 5/43, New Guinea) (NA-SC)

Above: A display of typical equipment carried in New Guinea. It includes a helmet and liner (camouflage-painted), inflatable rubber bladders, groundsheet, M1910 T-handled entrenching tool, M1943 jungle pack (OD) with mess kit, training gas mask, medical kit, camouflage jungle suit, matchbox with compass, small flashlight, rubberized food bags, gloves, machete, hunting knife and an M1928 Thompson submachine-gun. (41st Div, 2/43, New Guinea) (NA-SC)

Opposite page, top: One of the most useful inventions of the war was the DUKW (pronounced 'duck'). This was an amphibious 2½ ton truck which could swim out to a freighter, pick up a load of cargo, return to the beach and drive the load inland to the supply dump. It proved invaluable in locations where there were no docks or port facilities. Hanging from the tree are two jungle hammocks. (JG)

Above: Each heavy weapons company had eight M1917A1 heavy machine-guns. These water-cooled guns could fire for longer periods of time without a heat buildup that would jam the weapon. The heavy tripod was designed to provide a very stable platform for long-range firing. These men have fashioned a platform on an outrigger canoe to patrol the coast of an island. (GG)

Left: The LCI (Landing Craft, Infantry) was a small ship that could transport 188 men for about 2,000 miles. They were shallow-draft vessels which were designed to run up onto the beach and allow the men to disembark over two side ramps. The inside was filled with very cramped bunks, but no kitchen facilities. The troops had to eat uncooked combat rations. (JG)

Left: This is a typical company or battalion command post in the fighting on New Guinea - a small hole scooped out of the soil and covered with a shelter half. Field telephones connect the post to other positions, and a box of grenades is kept handy to repel any Japanese assault. (32nd Div. 11/42, New Guinea). (NA-SC)

Below: Captured Japanese weapons were popular souvenirs. The one man is examining a lightweight Japanese grenade launcher nicknamed the 'knee mortar'. Although the name was given because of its size, a number of G.I.s believed it was designed to be fired while being rested on the leg. If this was attempted, the recoil of the weapon risked shattering the unfortunate soldier's leg. Official warnings had to be issued to prevent the troops from trying this trick. (32nd Div. 11/42, New Guinea) (NA-SC)

Right: In later fighting on New Guinea, signalmen operate two SCR-300 backpack radios. This was the most successful radio of the war, as it could be carried and operated by a single man. It was commonly used to communicate between company and battalion headquarters, but a range of up to 20 miles and ease of portability made it invaluable for many different missions. (31st Div. 8/44, New Guinea) (NA-SC)

Right: Staff of the 3rd Battalion, 127th Infantry Regiment, stand in front of a Japanese bunker near Buna. The central individual's fatigues appear to have been over-dyed a darker green. The man wearing Marine Corps HBTs is probably a liaison officer attached from the Corps. On the left, holding a Thompson submachine-gun, is Colonel Swedberg, the battalion commander. (32nd Div.12/42, New Guinea) (NA-SC)

Left: Infantry regiments were authorized a cannon company to provide artillery support right up on the front lines. Some cannon companies used 75mm pack howitzers, others the M7 tracked 'Priest'. The 34th Infantry Regiment were issued these M8 howitzer motor carriages – a 75mm gun mounted on an M5 light tank chassis. (24th Div. 6/44, New Guinea) (NA-SC)

Left: Members of the 24th Division advance on Biak Island in Dutch New Guinea. The second man from the end wears boots that have been hobnailed. Hobnails were preferred as they gave better traction when climbing about in the jungle. Unfortunately, the wet climate caused the hobnails to rust quickly and fall out. In some areas leather boots lasted an average of ten days before rotting apart. (24th Division, 6/44, New Guinea) (NA-SC)

Right: These soldiers land near Aitape carrying the M1 carbine. The carbine was a lightweight weapon designed as a sidearm, not as a replacement for the Garand. In Europe the low power and lack of accuracy was a disadvantage, but in the dense Pacific jungles it proved an ideal weapon. The man in front has the special jungle first-aid kit attached to his belt, with the standard first-aid pouch hung underneath. (41st Div. 4/44, New Guinea) (NA-SC)

Right: M4A1 Sherman tanks of the 603rd Tank Company await orders after disembarking from an LST (Landing Ship, Tank) on Wake Island. No armored divisions took part in the Pacific war, but small units of tanks played a major role in helping the infantry destroy pillboxes and strongpoints. Compared with the Germans, the Japanese had very poor anti-tank weapons, so even a few tanks could make an important difference in a battle. (5/44, New Guinea) (NA-SC)

Opposite page: Even in Alaska, soldiers made their own camouflage uniforms. This member of the Kiska invasion force is applying paint to his HBT trousers and his Arctic field jacket. The Arctic jacket was a warmer variation of the M41 field jacket and can be identified by the wrist straps. (8/43, Kiska) (SC-NY)

Right: Colonel Robert Frederick, commander of the First Special Service Force, provides an excellent view of the paratrooper helmet. The FSSF had more specialized training (including parachuting) than any other U.S. Army unit. Frederick is shown here during the invasion of Kiska, with the Kiska Task Force patch on his right shoulder. There was bloody fighting to retake Attu, but the Japanese evacuated Kiska without a fight. (FSSF, 8/43, Kiska) (SC-NY)

Below: The Weasel was a small tracked vehicle originally designed to be used on snow. It proved to be reliable transport in most rugged conditions. Here a group of men is needed to help a weasel pull an anti-tank gun up a hill in the Aleutian Islands. The cold, wet weather of the Aleutians was in sharp contrast to the conditions encountered in other areas of the Pacific war. This was the only American territory occupied by an enemy in World War II. (8/43, Kiska) (SC-NY)

Left: With the Marines busy invading Tarawa, the 27th Division was given the task of landing on the nearby island of Makin. These men carry carbines and a Thompson submachine-gun. They wear the M1928 haversack along with two canteens. One soldier has a machete instead of a bayonet on his haversack. (27th Div. 11/43, Makin) (NA-SC)

Below left: Every squad had one BAR (Browning Automatic Rifle). This was a fully automatic, magazine-fed weapon. Although heavier than a Garand, it was generally popular. Many units tried to ensure that each squad was (unofficially) equipped with two BARs. The bipod and flash hider were often removed to cut down on the weight. (27th Div. 1/44, Makin,) (NA-SC)

Opposite page top: The new 'frog-skin' jungle suit is shown off by staff of a portable hospital. They also wear the newly designed jungle boots, which were essentially high-topped sneakers. The photograph was taken to illustrate the way these men had to hand-carry all their equipment into the jungle before suitable roads were built. (13th Portable Hospital, 5/43, New Guinea) (NA-SC)

Opposite page, bottom: Reinforcements for the 41st Division come ashore at Aitape, New Guinea. They all wear the camouflage version of the jungle pack. This pack was the only item of field gear issued to the Army that was made from camouflage material. All other web or canvas items were made in khaki or olive drab. (41st Div. 4/44, New Guinea) (NA-SC)

Left: Men of the 103rd Infantry Regiment gather in a bomb crater on New Georgia. Most of them are wearing the one-piece jungle suit. One man has opened the top to reveal the internal suspenders of the suit. This camouflage pattern worked when the wearer stayed still, but was ineffective when on the move. The one-piece design was disliked, and many of these suits were cut down into a jacket which was worn over standard HBT trousers. (43rd Div. 8/43, New Georgia) (NA-SC)

Left: Most of the signal company of the 43rd Division landing on New Georgia are still using the old M1928 haversack. The issue of camouflage uniforms appears to have been confined to the combat troops, with these headquarters troops retaining their standard HBTs. Even in July 1943 a few men carry the 1903 Springfield. A few machetes and bolos are hung on various packs. (43rd Div. 6/43, New Georgia) (NA-SC)

Right: An infantry captain on New Georgia is stripped down to his shorts and sits on a raincoat. His dog tags have been silenced with a rubber section cut from a gas mask hose. Numerous tropical skin diseases plagued the men on the islands and one of the only cures was to expose the affected area to sunlight whenever possible. When combat ended, many men took to sunbathing to heal their 'jungle-rot'. (8/43, New Georgia) (NA-SC)

Below: The ¾ ton Dodge weapons carrier was a very rugged four-wheel drive vehicle, but it was no match for the muddy roads on Munda. As soon as the area was cleared of Japanese, engineers moved in to construct a road made of crushed coral. Unlike the European Theater, engineers in the Pacific found they had to start from scratch – turning paths into roads and lagoons into ports. (8/43, Munda) (NA-SC)

Left: One of the élite units in the Pacific was the Alamo Scouts, who were the eyes and ears of the 6th Army. They performed numerous reconnaissance missions to gather valuable information. These four Alamo Scouts landed behind Japanese lines on the Philippines and spent five weeks radioing intelligence back to their headquarters. They all seem to favor the HBT cap and the newly developed 'double buckle' combat boot. (Alamo Scouts, 6/45, Luzon, PI) (NA-SC)

Left: Lieutenant General Walter Kruger (second from right), commander of the 6th Army, founder of the Alamo Scouts, is seen here examining a Japanese Hotchkiss heavy machine-gun at the Alamo Scouts training center. The lieutenant next to him wears the standard Alamo Scout uniform of HBT cap, khaki cotton shirt, HBT trousers and leggings. Leggings, although disliked, were mandatory due to the plagues of mosquitoes in the training camp area. (Alamo Scouts, 8/44, Hollandia) (NA-SC)

Top: The 6th Ranger Battalion was the only official U.S. Ranger unit to serve in the Pacific. Officers of the unit are seen here on New Guinea, in late 1944, wearing a fairly straightforward HBT uniform with leggings. The camouflage helmet covers were issued to the Army on a limited basis. The officer in charge wears the high leather paratrooper boot: a rare find the Pacific. (6th Ranger Bn. 10/44, Finschafen) (NA-SC)

Above: A column of 6th Rangers is shown on its way to rescue Allied POWs from the Cabanatuan prison camp in the Philippines. Over 500 prisoners were saved from possible execution by this daring behind-the-lines raid. The troops are carrying a very light amount of web gear and almost all wear the HBT cap. Helmets and packs have been left behind for this mission, but a number of men carry a shoulder-slung ammo bag. (6th Ranger Bn. 1/45, Luzon, PI) (NA-SC)

Left: The 11th Airborne was the only paratrooper division to serve in the Pacific. Shown here with Hollywood stars on a morale-building tour are men wearing the special M1942 para-trooper uniform and high paratrooper boots. This uniform had large pockets on both jacket and trousers. In the rear are two officers wear-ing caps tailor-made out of khaki material and nicknamed 'Swing' caps after the 11th A/B commander, General Joseph Swing. (11th A/B Div. 1944, New Guinea) (JG)

Left: The 158th Infantry Regiment was an Arizona National Guard unit that was sent to Panama for special jungle training. Many of the men were of American Indian ancestry. The unit became known as 'the Bushmasters'. In front are their two principal weapons: a Thompson submachine-gun and an M1903 Springfield rifle cut down for lighter weight. This was a modification specific to the Bushmasters. (158th Infantry Regiment, Panama) (TH)

Above: The most important operation that took place in Burma was the construction of the Ledo road. This road, cut through the foothills of the Himalayas, served as a vital supply line to Nationalist Chinese troops in desperate need of materials. Because much of the work took place at high altitudes, warm clothing, such as the M41 field jackets and mackinaws seen here, was vital. (1/45, Burma) (NA-SC)

Left: Among the many units of native troops used by the Americans in the China–Burma–India area were the Gurkha Rangers. These men were employed to guard an OSS (Office of Strategic Services) base camp. Other well-known local units were the Jingpaw and Kachin Rangers, all serving in Northern Burma. This Gurkha wears a standard U.S. wool shirt and trousers, but British-style puttees and boots. (Burma, 1/45) (NA-SC)

Right: Utilizing a local workforce such as these elephants allowed the G.I.s to make the most of limited resources. In some locations where every drop of gasoline had to be airlifted in from a great distance, elephants could be more effective than bulldozers. (1/45, Burma) (NA-SC)

Below: The most famous unit to serve in Burma was 'Merrill's Marauders'. These men made their way through heavy jungle to outflank Japanese defensive positions. Seen here taking a break by the side of a trail, they are wearing HBTs and leggings, but one man in the center wears the knit wool cap normally associated with colder climates. Extra wool material has been taped to the shoulder straps as makeshift padding. The Marauders carried all their supplies with them and received more only through drops from aircraft. (Merrill's Marauders, Burma) (NA-SC)

Left: An officer from the 81st Division, armed with a carbine, leaves a landing craft just behind his radioman who carries an SCR-300. On his right hip is the special jungle first-aid kit, with the standard first-aid kit hung below. All the men in this photograph are carrying two canteens and none are wearing leggings. (81st Div. 9/44, Ulithi) (NA-SC)

Left: Prior to the invasion of Palau, men from the 81st Division gather for a religious service on the deck of a transport. What is unusual is that most of the men have a tactical unit marking painted on the back of their HBT jackets. Most combat uniforms worn in the Pacific never displayed any patches or other unit insignia. It is possible that these markings were developed by the 81st Division and used only for a short period. (81st Div. 9/44, Palau) (NA-SC)

Right: Another wave of men from the 81st land on Ulithi in September 1944. The soldier on the right bears a tactical marking used by the 81st at this time. The central individual carrying the carbine wears the three-pocket grenade pouch, alongside a canteen and a jungle first-aid kit. The helmets are painted in an odd geometric camouflage pattern. (81st Div. 9/44, Ulithi) (NA-SC)

Right: On the island of Anguar stretcher-bearers bring a casualty to an aid station. The Red Cross is not prominently displayed, because the Japanese did not spare medical personnel or facilities. The small ammunition cart at right is now filled with cans of water, a much more valuable commodity in this hot region. (81st Div. 9/44, Ulithi) (NA-SC)

Left: A typical engineer reels out blasting wire to set off a charge in a coral pit. The coral gravel will then be used for a roadbed. Blasting wire was always a bright red color so that no one would mistake it for regular field telephone wire and accidentally tap into it. The engineer is wearing the first-pattern one-piece HBT suit and helmet liner. He has removed the attached belt from the HBT suit for added comfort. (118th Eng. Bn. 8/43, New Georgia) (NA-SC)

Opposite page, top: An infantry company had two M1919A4 light machine-guns such as this one in use on Kwajalein. The weapon has been camouflaged by rubbing it with coral dust. The helmet nets are unusual, as many units refused to allow their men to wear them. Most Japanese troops wore helmet nets, so it was one more way to tell the difference between friend and foe in dense jungle. (7th Div.2/44, Kwajalein) (NA-SC)

Opposite page, bottom: Men from a regimental cannon company move a 75mm howitzer inland on Kwajalein. The camouflage-painted helmets are a very distinctive pattern. Under their M1928 packs these men carry the lightweight gas mask bag – although in 1944 it was being used to carry extra supplies rather than gas masks. The last man on the right also carries a bazooka, which was a very effective weapon to employ against Japanese bunkers. (7th Div. 2/44, Kwajalein) (NA-SC)

Opposite page, top: A reconnaissance team from the 1st Cavalry Division after returning from a mission on Los Negros in May 1944. They all wear jungle boots and 'frogskin' jungle suit. The cap was never officially made in camouflage so they have hand-painted their HBT caps in a similar pattern. All are armed with the lightweight carbine. One man has the folding stock carbine that was designed for the paratroops. (1st Cav. Div. 6/44, Los Negros) (NA-SC)

Opposite page, bottom: The 37th Division Intelligence section on Guam was typical of office space in the Pacific. In Europe there was usually a building that could serve the purpose. Here in the Pacific, personnel sometimes even lacked

tents. The climate rotted tent canvas at an alarming rate and shelter was often impossible to find. The typist wears his leggings under rolled-up trousers in order to increase ventilation. (37th Div. 7/44, Marianas) (NA-SC)

Above: Both crewmen of this 81mm mortar wear the jungle pack (one in camouflage material). The machete strapped to one pack was invaluable for cutting through the dense jungle growth. Each man would carry a .45 caliber pistol for close defense. Only two men were needed to aim and fire the weapon, but the rest of the crew were needed to carry ammunition for it. (31st Div. 9/44, Morotai) (NA-SC)

Opposite page, top: Americal Division troops clog the Bougainville beaches as they reinforce Marines already fighting on the island. LVCPs are being used to bring men in from a larger ship. This photo shows why the Japanese made the landing beaches their prime target. This was the area where the greatest concentration of men and supplies would be found. (Americal Div. 1/44, Bougainville) (NA-NY)

Opposite page, bottom: Men from the Americal Division sort mail on Bougainville. One soldier has rolled back the cuffs of his jungle suit to expose the reversible brown pattern of the camouflage. Although by this time, in 1944, all socks and

underwear were supposed to have been dyed olive drab, this photograph shows that some white examples were still working their way out of the supply system. (Americal Div. 1944, Bougainville) (NA-SC)

Above: The M1 flamethrower was a difficult weapon to use. It had a short range of 30 yards and the operator had to brace himself against the strong backward thrust of the flaming jet. If a flamethrower could get close enough to a Japanese bunker it could either burn the occupants out, or the flame could exhaust all the oxygen and suffocate anyone inside. (37th Div. 3/44, Bougainville) (NA-SC)

Left: The men are taking cover from a Japanese sniper who has just opened fire. The burning jeep has been modified in the field to serve as a crude ambulance. The supports will hold two wounded men on stretchers. In the background are two M3 'Stuart' light tanks – armed with the small 37mm gun. (37th Div. 1944) (NA-SC)

Opposite page, bottom: Men from the 93rd Division haul mortar shells in the standard three-shell container across a Bougainville river. With no roads in the area, supplies had to be hand-carried up to the front lines. The 93rd, the only all African American division in the Pacific Theater, was frequently assigned to such non-combat duties, or split into small units supporting other divisions. (93rd Div. 1944) (NA-SC)

Below: Troops from the 93rd Division make their way through a muddy stretch of jungle. The first man in line wears an ammo bag as a pack, while the second man has an M3 trench knife and helmet slung from his jungle pack. He also carries an M1943 folding entrenching tool on his hip. The third soldier carries a web case which was designed to hold signal equipment. (93rd Div. 4/44) (NA-SC)

Above: The M7 'Priest' was a 105mm howitzer mounted on the chassis of a Sherman tank. This self-propelled howitzer was much more mobile than a gun towed by a truck. The armor allowed the crew protection from small arms when the gun moved up to the front lines to destroy a bunker. By the end of the war most Regimental cannon companies were equipped with this vehicle. (33rd Div, 3/45, Luzon, PI) (NA-SC)

Right: Troops of the 41st Division follow a Sherman tank advancing on Mindanao. Most of the men wear the camouflage version of the jungle pack. A mixture of M1943 folding shovels and the T-handled M1910 shovel are strapped to the packs. The tank crew is wearing the fiber tanker's helmet instead of a steel combat helmet. (41st Div. 3/45, Mindanao, PI) (NA-SC)

Opposite page, top: The 57mm anti-tank gun replaced the smaller 37mm gun in 1943. This gun is being put to good use firing at Japanese pillboxes in the Philippines. Unlike the war in Europe, most anti-tank weapons in the Pacific were used to destroy Japanese fortifications. The 57mm gun had a wavy-top gun-shield, while the 37mm shield was cut straight across. (38th Div. 5/45, Luzon, PI) (NA-SC)

Left: What the Army lacked in artillery support from its own guns was made up for by ships sitting off the coast. These men from a Joint Assault Signal Company relay requests for fire support from the infantry (coming in over the low-powered SCR-536 handheld radio), to the gun crews of battleships or cruisers. One man is running a portable generator to provide power for the stronger Navy radio. (293rd JASCO, 1/45, Luzon, PI) (NA-SC)

Opposite page, bottom: An air-ground liaison team attached to the 43rd Division on the Philippines controlled air strikes by carrier-based planes until local airstrips could be captured or built. On the right front fender of the jeep can be seen a chemical decontamination device, while the exhaust tube has been extended up on the right rear so that the jeep could be driven off a landing craft in high water. (1/45, Luzon, PI) (NA-SC)

Below: The U.S. Army had the best radios in the world, but it still relied heavily on telephone communication by wire. This BD-71 switchboard could handle six different lines and was perfect for battalion-level communications. The tags indicate the positions of the wires in case the equipment has to be moved or exchanged. The operator wears the canvas and rubber jungle boots and sits on a reel of phone wire. (1/45, Luzon, PI) (NA-SC)

Above: Strapped to this man's back is a machete, squad rifle cleaning kit, T-handled shovel and a black cardboard tube with metal ends. These tubes were used to ship all kinds of munitions from grenades to mortar shells. The DR-8 phone wire reel in front of him would be used with a lightweight sound-powered telephone. (10/44, Leyte, PI) (NA-SC)

Opposite page, top: Bulldozers supporting the 38th Division on the Philippines illustrate the difficulty of building roads in the jungle. Bulldozers were not only employed for construction jobs, but were frequently used as weapons against Japanese bunkers. They would plow dirt over the bunker openings, burying the occupants. The thick blade gave some protection from small-arms fire, but a number of dozers were given armored cabins to protect the operators. (113th Eng. Bn. 6/45, Luzon, PI) (NA-SC)

Right: A tank from the 716th Tank Battalion is pulled from a muddy river bottom by another M4 Sherman. It is unusual to see troops riding on tanks in the Pacific. Normally the men preferred to walk in protection behind the vehicle. Infantrymen felt very exposed riding in this manner, and liked to be able to take cover rapidly if fired upon. (Americal Div. 1945, Cebu, PI) (NA-SC)

Above: Major General Seibert, commander of X Corps, and Major General Irving, commander of the 24th Division, discuss plans. Seibert (left) wears the khaki cotton shirt and trousers with M1937 engineer rubber boots, while Irving wears the HBT uniform with rather dishevelled leggings. The wearing of rank insignia was rare in combat, as men feared they would be noticed by Japanese snipers. (24th Div. 10/44, Leyte, PI) (NA-SC)

Opposite page, top: Major General Swift, commander of I Corps, and Brigadier General MacNider, commander of the 158th Regimental Combat Team, and his staff. Second from right is Colonel Erle Sandlin who commanded the 158th Infantry Regiment (the Bushmasters). Swift wears a thin cot-

ton Navy shirt and a dust mask. The man at far right wears the first-pattern HBT jacket, Sandlin wears the one-piece HBT suit, and at far left is a second-pattern HBT jacket. (158th RCT, 1/45, Luzon, PI) (NA-SC)

Opposite page, bottom: An 11th Airborne Division paratrooper leads a mule carrying supplies down a Filipino road. Airborne units were not as well equipped with vehicles, so they often had to resort to field expedient transportation. The mule may have been an official issue, as animal transport was frequently used in rugged terrain. This paratrooper wears standard HBT fatigues instead of his paratrooper uniform. (11th A/B Div. 2/45, Luzon, PI) (NA-SC)

Opposite page, top: The crew of an M8 armored car lay out a colored aerial recognition panel. These brightly colored markers were used to show aircraft where friendly troops were located. The M8 is armed with a 37mm gun and both a .30 caliber and a .50 caliber machine-gun. This armored car was normally found in a division's reconnaissance troop. (37th Div. Luzon, PI) (NA-SC)

Left: An M10 tank destroyer with a 3-inch gun moves through a Philippine town. The M10 was an open-topped tank with a high velocity gun. Originally designed to defend against enemy tanks that might break through the lines, it was extremely effective against Japanese emplacements. (77th Div. 12/44 Leyte, PI) (NA-SC)

Above: There were three 60mm mortars in the weapons platoon of the rifle company. This mortar could easily be carried by one man and had a range of 2,000 yards. The high explosive shells stacked in front of the mortar (in the early yellow coloring) could be fired as fast as the loader could drop them down the tube. (Americal Div. Bougainville) (NA-SC)

Opposite page, top: The HBT cap seems to be the headgear of choice among these men. Originally the peaked HBT cap was issued only to mechanics and vehicle crews, with the rest of the troops getting the full-brim HBT hat. By the end of the war the cap appears to have become a more popular item. (24th Div. 4/45, Mindanao, PI) (NA-SC)

Opposite page, bottom: After four years overseas and six major operations against the Japanese, these two men have acquired some very nice souvenirs. The staff sergeant on the left wears his rank insignia on his HBT jacket. This was uncommon, as the HBT jacket was technically a work uni-

form and wearing insignia on it was against regulations. It was more usual to paint the rank stripes on HBTs in the field. (32nd Div. 8/45, Luzon, PI) (NA-SC)

Above: These medics are stabilizing a casualty so that he can be moved to a well-equipped hospital ship. Swift evacuation was the most important factor in saving a man's life. Note the two canteens and jungle first-aid kit on the rear of the one medic. His helmet, unlike the others, appears to have a faint camouflage pattern painted on it. (4/45, Philippines) (NA-NY)

Opposite page, top: These 77th Division troops have just been landed on the Ryukyus Islands by an amphibious vehicle known as an 'alligator'. The tracked alligator could climb over the coral reefs that ringed many of the Pacific islands. Even in 1945 these men are carrying the cumbersome M1928 haversacks. (77th Div. 3/45, Ryukyus) (NA-SC)

Opposite page, bottom: This shot of the 96th Division on Okinawa illustrates the baggy pockets of the later HBT trousers and the 'buckle' combat boots. The central figure has an M1919A6 machine-gun – essentially the same as the A4 tripod-mounted version, but the A6 has an added stock

and bipod. Judging by the number of ammo cans, this group is probably one of the two light machine teams in the weapons platoon. (96th Div. 1945, Okinawa) (NA-SC)

Above: In March 1945 the 77th Division troops were wearing division insignia painted on their helmets as shown in this photograph taken on Okinawa. This was only done at the very end of the war. In the center is an M1917A1 machine-gun with steam condensing tube wrapped around the barrel. Another man would carry the tripod, while the rest carried the ammo supply. (77th Div. 3/45, Okinawa) (NA-SC)

Above: A flamethrowing tank on Okinawa burns out a Japanese defensive position. By placing the flammable material inside the protection of a tank's armor, flamethrowers became less vulnerable to enemy fire. A tank could also carry a larger supply of flammable liquid and thus stay in action longer. (7th Div. 4/45, Okinawa) (NA-SC)

Below: Troops of the 77th Division on Okinawa listen to a radio report that Germany has surrendered and the war is over in Europe. They know that they still have to fight a long war in the Pacific. Note the adjustable neck opening in their ponchos. The latter did not replace raincoats until very late in the war. (77th Div. 5/45, Okinawa) (NA-SC)

Above: The older man in the center is news correspondent Ernie Pyle. Probably no civilian was more admired and loved by the fighting men. He spent his time living in foxholes and writing about the real war on the front line. Shortly after this photo was taken on Okinawa, he was killed by a Japanese sniper. Behind him can be seen the Marine Corps camouflage helmet cover. (4/45, Okinawa) (NA-NY)

Below: These men have been through every campaign in which the 77th Division has participated. The central medic carries the special medical aid bag. Normally medics would carry two such bags filled with medical supplies. The row of grommets enabled the bag, if not filled, to be laced up to a smaller size. (77th Div. 5/45, Okinawa) (NA-SC)

Above: Tokyo has a roughly similar climate to that of the Baltimore-Washington area, so these members of the occupation force had to be issued warm clothing. In this case they wear the M43 field jacket with hood, the M43 cap and buckle combat boots. One of the men examining this Japanese AA gun wears a 77th Division patch on his jacket. It was not until hostilities ceased that most units took to wearing their unit insignia. (77th Div. 10/45, Japan) (NA-SC)

Below: 'Red Arrow' men of the 32nd Division display unit insignia on their helmet liners, along with their ranks. It was uncommon to find such markings in the Pacific until the end of the war. Then, many units began to mark anything and everything with insignia. By this time they have been issued with the new buckle combat boot. The sign indicates the different campaigns these men have fought in. (32nd Div. 10/45, Japan) (NA-SC)

Above: Before being sent home, men from the Americal Division are informally presented their medals. The officer, with an Americal patch, wears the khaki cotton uniform. The men all wear the second-pattern HBT jacket had large unpleated jacket pockets. The third-pattern jacket had a large pleat in the pockets, while the fourth and final pattern reverted to a small shirt-type pocket. Only the first-pattern HBT jacket had the waist band with two buttons. (Americal Div. 10/45, Japan) (NA-SC)

Below: There is very little to indicate that these are para-troopers from the 11th Airborne Division, except their high paratrooper boots. They wear the M1944 pack composed of a small backpack with a detachable cargo bag underneath. It was based on the earlier Marine Corps pack. This equipment only began to be issued at the end of the war, and did not see widespread combat use. (11th A/B Div. 8/45, Kadena) (NA-SC)

The war in the Pacific produced great animosity between either side. In an unusual photograph an American provides a cigarette to a Japanese enlisted man at surrender talks held on top of the Sierra Madres in the Philippines. Japanese soldiers would continue to surrender to the Americans throughout the Pacific for years to come, the last being in 1975. (38th Div. 8/45, Luzon, PI) (NA-SC)